To a very special
TEACHER

WRITTEN BY PAM BROWN
ILLUSTRATED BY JULIETTE CLARKE

. . .

Thank you for making school

a place we love to go to

in the morning.

. . .

A HELEN EXLEY GIFTBOOK

⊟EXLEY

THANK YOU FOR EVERYTHING

Thank you for making learning not a job but a joy.

Thank you for making me feel valuable.

Thank you for helping me to discover what I do best
– and to do it even better.

Thank you for taking away the fear of things I could
not understand – and persuading me that
I understood them after all.

Thank you for untangling tangles.

Thank you for being someone I can always trust
– and turn to when life gets difficult.

. . .

Some teachers make passing exams and getting good
grades the only reason for learning.

Thank you for showing us that it can be fun.

. . .

Thank you for persuading me that I was better than
I suspected.

. . .

Thank you for never seeing mistakes as failures
– but as ways to learn.

. . .

It's as hard to be clever as to be a little slow.
Thank you for understanding all of us
and giving us the time and care each of us needs.

. . .

You never make us
feel you are just
stuffing us with facts.
Instead – you go <u>with</u>
us on voyages
of discovery.

. . .

<u>OPENING DOORS FOR US</u>

You have taught us to have adventures in our heads
– to search and discover, to live with amazement.

. . .

Good teachers can persuade their students that
learning is not an imposition, an interference, a theft
of freedom – but an excitement, and the key to a
greater freedom than they have ever known.

. . .

When you told us about the wise and the good and the clever, the thinkers and makers and dreamers – people who changed the world – you always reminded us that they were children once and had everything to learn.

It gave us the heart to try.

. . .

A class and a teacher who have just defeated a difficult problem beam at each other in delight. The air is full of invisible hugging.

. . .

A teacher takes the everyday things of life, the things a child knows, and fashions them into stepping stones of knowledge and growth.

. . .

A class bewitched by a problem, a discovery, an experience, fizzes like a firework and celebrates in stars!

. . .

WHAT KINDNESS MEANS

When every detail of what you taught has
been forgotten, enthusiasm,
encouragement and
kindness will remain.

. . .

Thank you for never being sarcastic
– the thing that baffles and
bewilders a child.

. . .

A good teacher gives the best job
– like feeding the tadpoles
or watering the plants –
to the saddest person.

A good teacher remembers being small
– and understands the terrors and the
sadnesses, the excitements and the joys of
the children in the class.

. . .

A good teacher knows when you
are very sad.
Even if you haven't said anything at all.
And lets you know you can tell her
all about it.
If you want to.

. . .

If a teacher really cares for her class,
it spreads.

LESSONS IN LIFE

Become good at anything and
you will love life more.
That's what you said.
And it's true.

. . .

A good teacher can help us make
something of our lives,
however bad times are.

. . .

People often hurt other people
because they don't understand
what it feels like.
You explained to us just how the
other people feel.

. . .

Thank you for showing us that we can learn from
failure, discover strength in difficulties,
find love and kindness in our darkest days.
Thank you for giving us the courage to use our
minds as well and as honestly as we can …
and never be afraid to question.
Thank you for showing us how to stand firm for
what we believe right … even when we are
shaking in our shoes.

. . .

You showed us it is perfectly all right to be ordinary
– because ordinary people aren't really
ordinary at all. Each one has something special they
can do. And every one is especially valuable to the
people that they love.
But – if you don't want to be ordinary –
you needn't be. Who knows what you can do if you
follow your special dream with all your heart and
mind and courage.

· ⚫ ·

A CLASSROOM LIKE AN OASIS

Whatever chaos reigned outside – we knew

we'd find order, justice and a chance to learn

inside your classroom.

And tolerance.

And laughter. And excitement.

. . .

A classroom can simply be an extension of

A Bad Area – or it can be an oasis.

. . .

Images of violence, anger and of

greed engulf us.

They hammer at the door.

But here we are safe.

In this small space we learn to value one

another, to think, to learn, to wonder,

to find peace and create.

You hold the ugliness and greed of the

world off – long enough for us to gather

strength to stand against them.

You show us the value of kindness.

You show us the power of patience,

of courage, of dedication.

You give us the chance to live.

. . .

HAPPY, LEARNING, ACHIEVING

One Monday you said,

"<u>Now</u> I understand. You explained that very well."

One Tuesday you said,

"Great Heavens – that is beautiful. How did you get

that luminous effect...?"

One Wednesday you said,

"Could you make a copy of your poem for me to keep?"

One Thursday you said,

"Come out in front and show the class."

One Friday you said,

"Thank you. That was very, very kind."

And so gave five small children gifts to last a lifetime.

. . .

There's a sort of buzz in a happy, learning

classroom. And we have it.

. . .

You never shoved us up an unexplored rockface –
whether it was geography, history,
computer studies, algebra or poetry. Or real granite.
You showed us the toeholds and finger holds. You
carefully guided us and made us feel absolutely safe
as we climbed. And when we finally reached the top,
you rejoiced with us at the view and the victory.

. . .

You put beauty into my hand.
And that was my beginning.
You, as my teacher, gave me words, images, ideas
from which to build my life.
Whatever I build, you helped to lay the foundations.

. . .

I LIKE TEACHERS . . .

who write clearly on the board,

who admit when they've made a mistake,

who read our stories with lots of

different voices,

who don't mind when you sing off key –

just so long as you are enjoying

the singing,

who smile a lot,

who would rather be a little ordinary than

always bossy and powerful,

who have little catchphrases like "lots of

hush now please" or "all I want to hear

now is the scuttle of pens."

. . .

I like teachers who understand when I
don't understand. And explain things
clearly. And notice when I put my hand
up. And listen quietly to my problems.
And give me a turn at feeding the hamster.
And smile when I've tried hard. And cheer
and clap when our play is over. And tell
us interesting things and give us
interesting things to do.

. . .

I like teachers who don't mind going over
their explanations again.
And again. And again.

. . .

Other people have nightmares about crocodiles or getting lost. For the poor teachers, it's parents.

. . .

PITY THE POOR TEACHER!

Words to strike ice in the teacher's heart:

"My dad says …"

"Miss. Emily's swallowed a button …"

"Sir. My arm has gone all spotty."

"My grandma wants to visit you about reading."

"Miss. Weren't we meant to be in the Hall this lesson?"

. . .

Teachers do not wake in the night from a dream of
pursuing wolves, wild-eyed and desperate.
They dream they have left all the
school projects on a bus.

. . .

A teacher is expected to deal with children that have
defeated their parents, their doctor, a
psychiatrist or two and a gaggle of social workers.
They are usually told that all that's needed is a
Normal Classroom Environment.

. . .

A schoolteacher has an unerring capacity to
discover spots, splinters, temperatures,
ringworm, nits and worse.
And to smile reassuringly.

. . .

A good teacher is not too thrown when
someone brings in a pet snake as
Something to Talk About.

<u>A GOOD TEACHER . . .</u>

One good teacher can change the world.

. . .

A good teacher notices when a child is trying
– even if the results are minute.
And shows she's seen the change.

. . .

A good teacher sees that everyone gets a turn at the
interesting jobs – and at the grotty ones.

. . .

Great careers can often be traced back to the
influence of one teacher.

. . .

A good teacher knows a word of praise can bring
sunlight to the gloomiest day.

. . .

A good teacher can look at a page of writing that
looks like tangled knitting and figure out what
you're trying to say.
She doesn't rewrite it.
She just gives it a sort of shake
– and it all falls into place.

. . .

A good teacher is as pleased as you are when, at last,
you succeed.

. . .

ALWAYS GUIDING, ENCOURAGING

You know that everyone has to begin at the very
beginning. And that a child is not stupid if he
or she has not been told or shown
how to do a thing.

You make learning an adventure – instead of a
forced march.

You take us a step at a time, at a speed that suits us.

And if some of us discover we can move forward in
leaps and soaring flight – you are delighted.

And if some of us plod gently but happily along the
path – that gives you equal pleasure.

. . .

A good teacher does not whistle for you to follow.

Does not shove you from behind.

A good teacher walks beside you – lets you explore,

invent, create, question, explain.

With a hand ready to steady you over

the stony places

– but only if you're really stuck.

A good teacher says, "Look."

"Think." "Try."

"What would happen if we tried it the

other way round?"

"Show me how to do it."

. . .

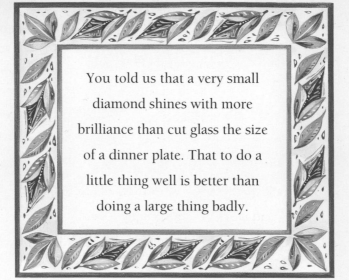

You told us that a very small
diamond shines with more
brilliance than cut glass the size
of a dinner plate. That to do a
little thing well is better than
doing a large thing badly.

VALUES FOR LIFE

The most important thing you have taught us
is that we all need one another.

. . .

You taught us that excellence costs.
Everyone has to decide just how much they are
prepared to pay.

. . .

A good teacher shows you how much you can do on your own – and how much more you can do working with others.

. . .

Thank you for making us value the differences between people instead of fearing them.

. . .

You taught us that if we want to do something very much, and work at it, and enjoy it and become better at it – then it doesn't much matter if we become famous or not.

. . .

You assured us that the great scientist and the great artist were once as little as we are and made mistakes and got confused.

. . .

You were the one who explained that a life can be as thin and flat as paper – or deep as the ocean and as high as the sky. We have to choose.

I WILL REMEMBER

You had a way with things.

The class will never forget you.

Neither will I.

. . .

School is a trial run for the world and a teacher can
only do so much to help us through it.

But teachers try.

They do their best.

And better than their best.

And we, free at last and eager to be off, say goodbye
with kindly arrogance and walk away.

Not knowing that you are a part of us forever.

. . .

Teachers are remembered more for what they were
than what they taught.

. . .

I will remember you always and always.

. . .